Leicester

IN OLD PHOTOGRAPHS

Clock Tower, *c.* 1930. In the centre of modern Leicester is the clock tower built in 1868 by Joseph Goddard. The statues on the tower, carved by Samuel Barfield, represent Simon de Montfort, William Wyggeston, Sir T. White and Alderman Newton. The foundation stone was laid by Mr John Burton, proprietor of the *Leicestershire Mercury*, who was largely responsible for raising the necessary funds by voluntary public subscriptions. King George V raised Leicester to city status in 1910.

Leicester

IN OLD PHOTOGRAPHS

Collected by DAVID R. BURTON

Alan Sutton Publishing Limited
Phoenix Mill · Far Thrupp
Stroud · Gloucestershire

First published 1993 in collaboration with
Leicestershire Museums, Arts & Records Service

Cover illustration: Eastgate, c. 1925.

British Library Cataloguing in Publication Data

A catalogue record for this book is available from
the British Library

ISBN 0–7509–0270–1

Typeset in 9/10 Sabon.
Typesetting and origination by
Alan Sutton Publishing Limited.
Printed in Great Britain by
Redwood Books, Trowbridge.

This milkman, pictured on his round
in about 1933, worked for Kirby and
West Dairymen.

Contents

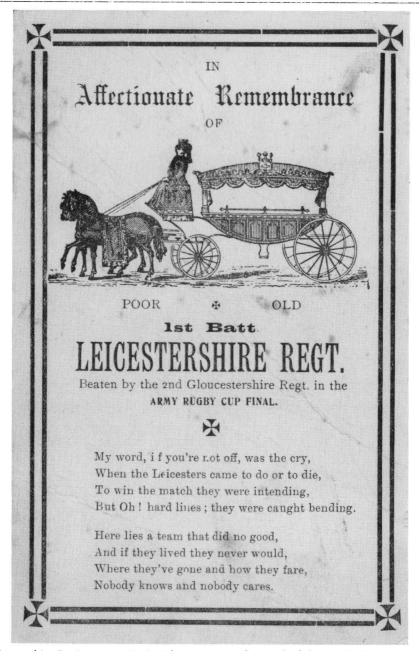

IN

Affectionate Remembrance

OF

POOR ✠ OLD

1st Batt.

LEICESTERSHIRE REGT.

Beaten by the 2nd Gloucestershire Regt. in the
ARMY RUGBY CUP FINAL.

✠

My word, i f you're r.ot off, was the cry,
When the Leicesters came to do or to die,
To win the match they were intending,
But Oh ! hard lines ; they were caught bending.

Here lies a team that did no good,
And if they lived they never would,
Where they've gone and how they fare,
Nobody knows and nobody cares.

Leicestershire Regiment, *c.* 1910. A humorous card typical of those which were popular in the early part of the century.

Introduction

About ten years ago I started to collect old picture postcards of Leicester and twelve months ago I decided it was time to share them with others. At about this time I was asked whether I would like to produce a book and this is the culmination of my efforts. Most of the pictures included are postcards and are from my collection and that of Trevor Hickman. Up until 1894 only official postcards could be sent through the post. From 1 September 1894, however, privately printed postcards could be sent, and F.T. Corkett of Leicester was one of the first of many to produce postcards for this purpose.

I have very fond memories of my childhood in Leicester. I lived on Wyngate Drive and can remember most of the neighbours and shopkeepers: Mr and Mrs Craston, the grocers, Miss Brown, the newsagent, Mrs Bamford, the greengrocer, the shops on Hinckley Road, Rawsons, Heards, Silvers, the Brooklyn Café, Hedges, and Skerritts. Then there were the trams, Hinckley Road School (with Mr Grudgings, the headmaster, Miss Jarvis, Miss Benson and Miss Walker), the allotments in Gimson Road (and falling in the pond), the Co-Operative Model Dairy (and watching the bottling machines). Memories! What a rich childhood we had! Dr Mann kept his surgery on the corner of Hinckley Road and Westcotes Drive.

During the war there was a shelter in the back garden and on the traffic island on Hinkley Road. 'Got any gum, chum?' we shouted at the convoys of American soldiers, and packets would be thrown in our direction. St Anne's cubs and scouts, the Revd E.W. Platt, and friends Wendy Dean and Jill Spring (both now sadly gone), sledging on the Western Park or playing in the 'gullies', roller-skating on the road and hanging onto the horse-drawn milk floats.

I left King Richard III School on Western Park and met work colleagues Ossey Gibson, Peter Nott, Brian Warner (Jack), Roy Finn (Errol) and George Moore, all at Knight's men's shop. There was time spent working for Whitcher Menswear with Peter Shoreland, Gordon Grouse, Pop Newman, Miss Hardy, Miss Dunham and Eric Stokes, trips to the Palace Theatre, the Odeon, the Gaumont, the Roxy, the Westleigh and the Olympia, walks in the parks, boating in Abbey Park and the peacocks.

My father went to the Middle East for five years in 1940 and on his return rejoined his old company, R. Morley & Sons. He was well known in the furniture trade and became Morley's funeral director. He died three years ago aged eighty-seven.

This collection is in no way a complete picture. I make no apologies for this. No one could do justice to Leicester in the past in one small book. I have tried to bring back memories, some happy, some sad, and I hope that most readers will enjoy looking back with pride at Leicester in old photographs.

Factories and Businesses

VIEW OF HARRISON & SONS' WELFORD ROAD WAREHOUSE, LEICESTER.

Harrison & Sons, *c.* 1910. This postcard advertises the Royal Midland Seed Warehouse in Welford Road. The message reads, 'We beg to acknowledge your esteemed order just to hand, which shall have our careful attention in due course. Soliciting a continuance of your favours, we are yours obediently, Harrison & Sons.'

CAPTAIN LESLIE CORAH,
4th Batt. Leicestershire Regiment,
Killed in action in France,
13th October, 1915.

Captain Leslie Corah, 4th Battalion Leicestershire Regiment. He was killed in action at Hohenzollern Redoubt in France on 13 October 1915. Captain Corah was a member of the well-known Leicester Hosiery Company and he fought alongside his fellow workers. Thirty-nine employees also lost their lives.

The Globe Inn, Silver Street was a well-known rendezvous for stockingers who had goods to sell of a hosiery nature. Probably the first trading done by a member of the Corah family was carried on here. From this small beginning started the Corah business, now known nationwide. St Margaret's and St Michael labels are synonymous with quality and fashion.

A letter dated 1868, quoting the motto of the Corah company and family.

The Corah family had lived in Leicestershire for 300 years before the Battle of Waterloo. Born in 1777, Nathaniel Corah, a native of Bagworth, worked as a mechanic in a gun factory in Birmingham. His father was a farmer and framework knitter. Nathaniel chose to learn the trade of framesmith. While he worked and lived in Birmingham, his wife and children lived in St Nicholas Street. He returned in 1815 and started the business now known throughout the world. The flat-frame pictured belonged to Nathaniel Corah. He died aged fifty-five in 1832.

High Street, c. 1945, showing Corts the ironmongers, Swears and Wells, and the tram stop where we caught the Hinckley Road tram. I remember the hot-potato man on cold evenings.

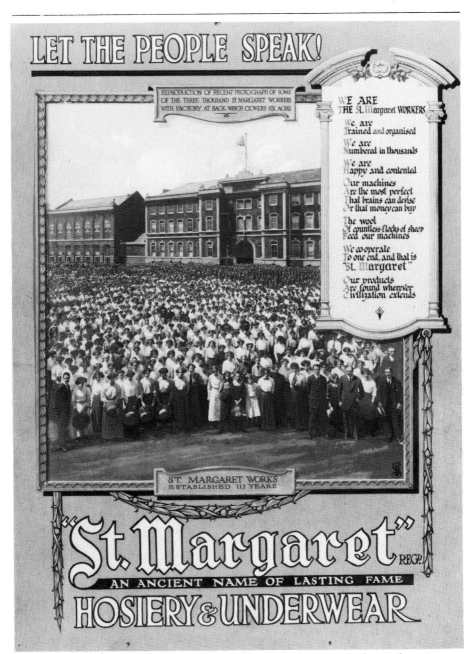

St Margaret Works. Some of the 3,000 workers are pictured outside the works 112 years after the start of Corahs. The factory covered an area of six acres.

The Leicester Boot Repairing Co., No. 2 Gower Street, off Belgrave Gate, *c.* 1900. It was known as Cooper & Co. Boot Manufacturer.

The Lambert Manufacturing Company. This business was started in 1910 in Friar Lane by Mr 'Fred' and Mr 'Harry' (Lambert), as they were known. They rented premises in the Exchange Building in Rutland Street as wholesalers in hosiery, etc., not long afterwards starting to manufacture on their own account. In 1923 they moved to Millstone Lane where Mr Ted Chawner, Miss Isabelle Porter, Miss Louise Riley and Miss Esther Chard joined the company, and the famous 'Milestones' trade mark appeared.

Mr Ted Chawner was born in Beaumanor Road, Belgrave, c. 1910, and worked for Hart & Levy before joining the Lambert Manufacturing Co. He was a keen radio ham and his call sign, G3DGV, was known in many countries. He retired after thirty-six years with the company.

The third floor workroom at Lamberts with Mr E.N. 'Ted' Chawner, factory manager, in the background on the left.

A. Whitcher & Co. Ltd, *c.* 1905. This postcard shows the front of the popular men's outfitters, known for many years as The Magnet. Mr Arthur Whitcher came from the Isle of Wight at the turn of the century. He had two sons, Walter and Stanley, who continued the business. Mr Walter had two sons, Michael and Tony, who have continued the family company. Mr Arthur Whitcher lived at Villars, Guilford Road.

Mr Frederick Richard Morley lived at 34 Friar Lane and owned the R. Morley & Sons drapers shop in Cheapside. He later moved to a new house built by Mr James Morley of Oxford Street in 1870. The Morley family lived there until 1914.

R. Morley & Son, est. 1828. The family originated from Thomas Morley (spelt Moorley in 1680) of East Bridgford near Nottingham. His grandson, Christopher Morley, baptized at Hawton near Newarke in 1735, was an agriculturist who won gold medals for farm management. Richard Morley, the eldest son of Christopher, was the father of the founder of the Morley business in Leicester, also called Richard. Richard was educated in Melton Mowbray and apprenticed to Hanman and Wright, linen drapers of Nottingham. In 1828 he founded the business of Morley and Wright. Ten years later he came to Leicester and opened the Cheapside shop. In 1863 the company expanded into the carpet trade, eventually moving to Cank Street in 1883. Richard died in 1884, aged eighty, and his two sons, F.R. Morley and John Morley, carried on the company. Mr John died in 1894. The premises in the market place were acquired in 1897 and customers could walk through to Cank Street. Mr F.R. Morley died in 1911 aged seventy-seven.

Richard Morley Huntrods, a son of F.R. Morley's eldest daughter, joined the staff in 1919 and became a partner some years later. The company was taken over by Maple & Co. in 1950. They moved to Granby Street in 1960.

The Morley family house at 44 Princess Road, built by Mr James Morley in 1870. It was purchased by Toc H in 1925 with the Revd H.H.F. Sawbridge as chaplain and secretary.

R. Morley staff, *c.* 1928. Back row, left to right: Mr Charles Warren (buyer, Manchester department), Mr James Everitt (buyer, ladies lingerie), Mr Cyril B. Day (accounts manager), Mr R.A. Burton (salesman), Mr F. Wright (funeral director), Mr Reg H. Jones (carpet sales), Mr Richard Huntrods (director), Mr Jack Marriott (buyer, soft furnishings), Mr Christopher Morley. Front row: Mr Alfred J. Perryman (buyer, carpet department), Mr Richard Morley (director), Mr S. Weller (buyer, furniture), Mr F. Henry Morley (director), -?-.

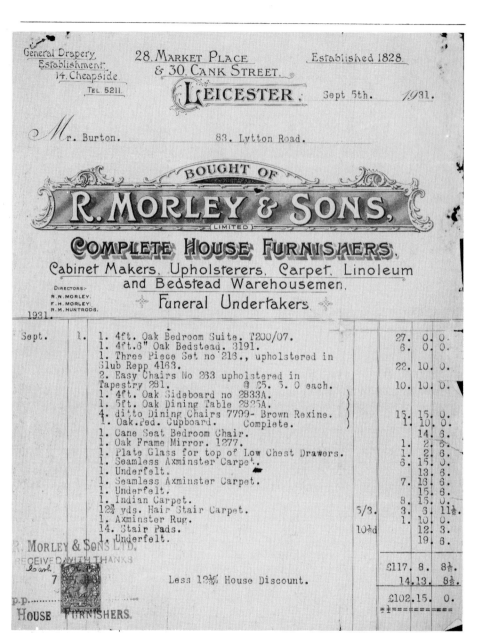

28. MARKET PLACE
& 30. CANK STREET,
Established 1828.

LEICESTER ;

Sept 5th. 1931.

Mr. Burton. 83. Lytton Road.

BOUGHT OF
R. MORLEY & SONS,
(LIMITED)

COMPLETE HOUSE FURNISHERS,
Cabinet Makers, Upholsterers, Carpet, Linoleum and Bedstead Warehousemen,
DIRECTORS:-
R.N. MORLEY.
F.H. MORLEY.
R.M. HUNTRODS.

❖ Funeral Undertakers ❖

1931.

					£	s	d
Sept.	1.	1. 4ft. Oak Bedroom Suite. 200/07.			27.	0.	0.
		1. 4ft.6" Oak Bedstead. 3191.			6.	0.	0.
		1. Three Piece Set no 216., upholstered in Slub Repp 4163.			22.	10.	0.
		2. Easy Chairs No 263 upholstered in Tapestry 291. @ £5. 5. 0 each.			10.	10.	0.
		1. 4ft. Oak Sideboard no 2833A.	)				
		1. 5ft. Oak Dining Table 2825A.	)				
		4. ditto Dining Chairs 7799- Brown Rexine.	)		15.	15.	0.
		1. Oak.Ped. Cupboard. Complete.	)		1.	10.	0.
		1. Cane Seat Bedroom Chair.				14.	6.
		1. Oak Frame Mirror. 1277.			1.	2.	6.
		1. Plate Glass for top of Low Chest Drawers.			1.	2.	6.
		1. Seamless Axminster Carpet.			6.	15.	0.
		1. Underfelt.				13.	6.
		1. Seamless Axminster Carpet.			7.	16.	6.
		1. Underfelt.				15.	6.
		1. Indian Carpet.			8.	15.	0.
		12¾ yds. Hair Stair Carpet.	5/3.		3.	6.	11½.
		1. Axminster Rug.			1.	10.	0.
		14. Stair Pads.	10½d			12.	3.
		1. Underfelt.				19.	6.
					£117.	8.	8½.
		Less 12½% House Discount.			14.	13.	8½.
					£102.	15.	0.

R. MORLEY & SONS LTD.
RECEIVED WITH THANKS

7

p.p...........

HOUSE FURNISHERS.

The bill for furnishing a house in 1931: less than £120! Many of these items are still in the Burton family.

R. Morley & Sons' drapery shop in Cheapside. R. Morley & Sons also had a furniture shop in the market which went through to Cank Street. During the war the market place shop became the Victory V Club.

Walter Ross Bakery, *c.* 1880. This is a wood engraving of 14 Framland Street, Upper Conduit Street.

W.T. Jee (*c.* 1904) were monumental masons (established 1849) in Rutland Street, at Nos 29 and 51. The business was run by Mrs Elizabeth Ann Jee.

WHAT WILL THIS COST PRINTING?

This question fully answered by return of post on application to

WINKS & SON,
STEAM PRINTING WORKS,
LEICESTER.

All kinds of BOOK WORK, REPORTS, PAMPHLETS, SERMONS, &c., printed in good new type, on superior paper, stitched and cut ready for use at the following rates :—

DESCRIPTION.	250 £ s. d.	500 £ s. d.	1000 £ s. d.
Long Primer leaded.			
16 pages. 8vo. Foolscap .... 6½ X 4¼	1 12 6	2 0 0	2 10 0
16 ,, 8vo. Crown .... 7¼ X 4¾	2 2 6	2 10 0	3 3 0
16 ,, 8vo. Demy .... 8⅜ X 5⅝	2 12 6	3 0 0	3 17 6

WINKS & SON,
STEAM PRINTING WORKS
53, HIGH STREET, LEICESTER,

Undertake Printing of every description to any extent, and suggest the followiug, trusting that it will induce those who know the Firm individually to favour them with their orders :—

Circulars	Catalogues	Cheque Books
Note Headings	Trade Price Lists	Law Printing
Prospectuses	Advice Notes	Memorandum Notes
Cards	Pamphlets	Post Cards
Handbills	Subscription Lists	Mercantile Printing of
Posting Bills	Club Rules	every description
Billheads	Reports of Societies	Printing for Societies,
Labels	Magazines	Institutions, &c.

Their Office is large and well furnished, and they are enabled to produce work at a fair and reasonable price. Estimates furnished.

H

A lovely example of an advertisement of *c.* 1881. Winks & Son were at 53 High Street, Leicester. The Co-Op was soon to take over this address.

Ride Clyde Cycles.

CLYDE Nº I, LADY'S CYCLE.
FITTED WITH WAIT'S PATENT RIM BRAKE.

PRICES:

GENTLEMEN'S.				LADIES'.		
No. 1	...	£14 14 0	No. 1	...	...	£15 0 0
Model A	...	£12 12 0	Model A	...	...	£13 0 0
No. 2	...	£10 10 0	No. 2	...	...	£10 10 0

Our **£10 10 0** (Lady's or Gentleman's) Bicycle is a Speciality, and will compare favourably with many other makes sold at much higher prices.

THE BEARINGS OF ALL OUR MACHINES ARE GUARANTEED TWO YEARS.

We can Repair any make of Machine, and Re-Plate and Re-Enamel at Lowest Prices, consistent with Best Work.

FIRST-CLASS MACHINES for Hire by the Hour, Day, Week or Month.

We are able to undertake all kinds of Gold and Silver Plating, Coppering, Lacquering or Bronzing, including Harness and Carriage Sets, Lamps, Spoons, Forks, Waiters, Urns, Tankards, Tea Sets, etc.

CLYDE LIGHT MOTOR CAR for 1901... ..Price £145.
Simplest, Neatest and Best of its kind. Can be driven by a lady after 1 hour's tuition. FURTHER PARTICULARS on application.

SOLE AGENTS FOR HUMBER CYCLES AND MOTORS.
ILLUSTRATED LISTS Post Free.

CLYDE CYCLE & MOTOR CAR Co., Ltd.,
Works: SHENTON STREET (Near Humberstone Rd. Mid. Rly.)
Show Rooms: LONDON ROAD, LEICESTER.

Clyde Cycles, 1901. The price of a car then – £145. What price today? And how sexist: 'Can be driven by a lady after 1 hour's tuition'!

Clock Tower and Cheapside, Leicester.

The corner of Cheapside and Eastgates, *c.* 1900.

Market Street, *c.* 1916. Herrington's were drapers, milliners and ladies outfitters. Their address was 18, 22, 24 & 26 Market Street. Mr Frederick Herrington lived at 22 Victoria Park Road.

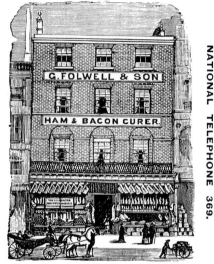

G. FOLWELL & SON,

HAM AND BACON CURERS, LARD REFINERS, &c.

Pies, Sausages, and Polonies.

MARKET PLACE, LEICESTER.

NATIONAL TELEPHONE 369.

Telegraphic Address:—"FOLWELL, LEICESTER.

Another fine advertisement (*c.* 1901) for arguably one of the best pie and sausage makers in the county.

Loseby Lane, *c.* 1907. Bell & Co. Drapers were on the corner of Town Hall Lane and Loseby Lane. Bell & Gimson are on the first floor.

SECTION TWO

People

Daniel Lambert. Described as a convivial native of Leicester, he was town gaoler. He measured 3 ft 1 in round the leg, 9 ft 4 in round the body and weighed 52 stone 11 pounds. He died on 21 June 1809 and is buried at Stamford.

PC Stephens, *c.* 1907. Weighing over 24 stone, PC Stephens was aged forty-eight when he died on 4 April 1908. He served for twenty-two years with the Leicester Police Force and was England's heaviest constable. He also served his country in the Zulu War in 1879.

The statue of John Biggs in Welford Place is by G.A. Lowson and was presented in 1871. John Biggs was Mayor of Leicester and a Member of Parliament.

A picture of Miss Woods outside her aunt's house at No. 83 Lytton Road, Clarendon Park, c. 1930.

A Midsummer Night's Dream at Hinckley Road School (Dovelands), *c.* 1946. Back row, left to right: Peter Parker, John Blanchard, David Milner, Colin Taylor and Donald Bateman. Middle row: Beryl Faulkner, David Royal, Ann Dyer, Keith Lacey and Sheila Bettles. Front row: Peggy Johnson, Janet Emery, Carole Moore and Pamela Yell.

Wyngate Drive, *c.* 1944. The rear garden of No. 103, the author's home from 1935 to 1958. Back row, left to right: Dorothy, Margaret and Kathleen Woods. Middle row: John Pether, Ian Grey, Donald Grey, -?-, and John Sewell. Front row: John Burton.

VJ Street Party, Wyngate Drive, 1945. Among those pictured are: Edmond Dalby, John Pether, Brian Chawner, John Sewell, Judy Taylor, Donald Grey, Janet Emery, Jennifer Hill, Michael Twigger, Molly Chawner, John Reader, Judith Sewell, Glenda Sharpe, Christine Reader and the author.

St Anne's Scouts, *c.* 1945, pictured outside their church on Letchworth Road. Scout leader was Major Locke. Back row, left to right: Alan Bridgewater, Ian Grey, Roger Green, David Allan, -?-, Peter Dowling and Pether Hockey. Middle row: J. Tuckwood, Bobby Small, Raymond Sharpe, John Sewell and John Pether. Seated: Stuart Oates, P. Markham, John Eley ('Q'), Major Locke ('Skip'), John Chivers ('Bosun'), Spud Thorne, John Baker and Michael Potter. Front row: Peter Bax, -?-, Patrick Gedney, David Milner, Brian Povoas, Michael Allen and Donald Grey.

SECTION THREE

Education

Wyggeston School, *c*. 1906. No. 17 Friar Lane was leased for the Junior School where boys were admitted in 1913. In 1915 the school moved to No. 11 The Newarke.

THE WYGGESTON GRAMMAR SCHOOL FOR GIRLS, LEICESTER.

Nov. 1947

This shows just a small section of the Wyggeston School photograph of 1947. The actual photograph is about 36 in long. Among the staff are Miss Durnford (deputy needlework), Miss Bird and Mrs Irons. The headmistress was Miss Nora Caress.

The Wyggeston Grammar School for Girls, Humberstone Gate, c. 1910. It is described on the back of the postcard as an 'advanced grade school'.

Wyggeston School. The September term began in the New Regent Road building, although it was not officially opened until 16 November. The building had been started in 1926, the foundation stone laid by Sir Jonathan North. Miss Nora Caress was head from 1927 until 1948, when Miss Myra E. Pedley took over until 1973. Miss Caress died in 1961. Miss Josephine E. Spencer became head in 1974.

The first Wyggeston School was opened on 17 June 1878 for the reception of pupils. It was then called the Wyggeston Hospital Schools. The headmistress was Miss Ellen Leicester. Ten years later it became the Wyggeston High School for Girls. Miss Leicester died in 1915. She was succeeded as head in 1903 by Miss Sarah Heron until 1927. Miss Heron died in August 1940.

The School of Art & Technology, *c.* 1930. Now known as the Hawthorn building, it was built by Everard and Pick in 1896–7 with additions in 1909, 1928 and 1937.

The Belgrave National Schools, *c.* 1905.

Narborough Road School, *c.* 1910, now Southfields College of Further Education, Westcotes Annexe. The architect was Leicester-born Edward Burgess. The postcard was sent to Blakeney, Gloucestershire from 18 Norman Street. One of the people on it is 'Sydney's Uncle Arthur' (mentioned on the card)! The author spent part of his schooldays here when Mr Vann was headmaster.

Narborough Road School, *c.* 1920. In 1947 this was a secondary modern school. Mr Vann was head, Mr Lewis taught woodwork and Mr Gabitas sport. Mr Vann played lead violin in the Leicester Symphony Orchestra.

Narborough Road School, *c.* 1910. The postcard shows the main hall. A small stage was added later and the author remembers the top left classroom as 1A. Among his schoolmates were Malcolm and Barry Richards, John Sewell, Ben Alexander, Tony Greasley and Barry Oakley. Some of them were members of the school orchestra and played in assembly.

Granby Road School, Aylestone. Miss May Read and Class 2, *c.* 1907.

Six teachers at Granby Road School, Aylestone, *c.* 1907. Standing, left to right: Miss Brown, Miss Hawell. Seated: Miss Coleman, Miss Louise George, the headmistress, -?-. Centre front: Miss May Read.

Entertainment and Leisure

The Palace Theatre, Belgrave Gate, and behind it the Floral Hall, *c*. 1912. The old carrier's cart and ornamental lamp-post all bring back memories.

The Royal Opera House in Silver Street, c. 1900. It was a treat to be brought here to see the pantomime. The Opera House was built by T.T. Paget but was originally much beyond the needs of Leicester.

During the Pageant of Leicester between 16 and 29 June 1932 Mr P. Groves and Mrs G. Cant dressed as the Prince and Princess of Wales for the opening of the Abbey Park. The park was originally opened on Whit Monday 1882.

The Floral Hall and Leicester Palace Theatre in Belgrave Gate, *c.* 1920, built in 1900 by architect Frank Matcham. The first doorway was the entrance to the Floral Hall and customers had to walk down a long passage to the cinema. The Palace Theatre put on variety shows. It closed in 1959/60 and was demolished.

De Montfort Hall, *c.* 1939. Built in 1913 and designed by Shirley Harrison, it has been described as a first rate concert hall. As a former member of the Leicester Operatic Society, I have performed here.

De Montfort Hall interior, *c.* 1939. This postcard shows some sort of meeting, although there is also a band on the stage.

Miss Florence Blackwell of the
Leicester Operatic Society in *Merrie
England*, *c.* 1905.

Mr Alfred Page of the Leicester
Operatic Society in *Merrie England*,
c. 1905.

Part of the historical pageant held in the Victoria Park on Coronation Day, 22 June 1911.

A tranquil scene beside the Aylestone Boat House on the River Soar at Aylestone, *c.* 1920.

SECTION FIVE
Transport

Belgrave Laundry, *c.* 1906. The location is probably in the Belgrave Road area. The driver is Harry Veal and his son Dick is on the footboard. The van boy is Bill Flint.

One of Leicester's first buses, *c.* 1899, owned by the Leicester Motor Company, a private firm.

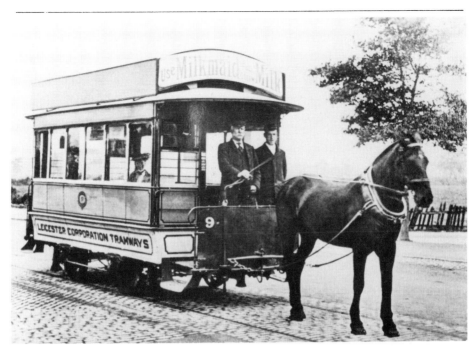

A horse tram, *c.* 1902. The tramways were started in 1872 by Messrs L. Turner, C. Stretton and W. Barfoot who had promoted tram companies in Leeds and Liverpool. The first route was from the clock tower to Belgrave.

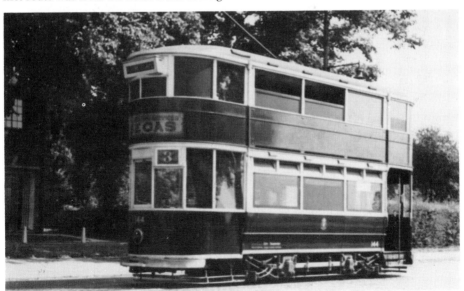

Tram car No. 144 at Stoneygate Terminus, *c.* 1940. There were around eighteen of this type with a 7 ft wheelbase. The standard car had a 6 ft wheelbase.

Town Hall, *c.* 1905, looking down Horsefair Street. The horse and cart is typical of those used by the railway goods department from Queen Street.

Tram 19 on the East Park Road route around the time of the First World War. The conductress is Mrs A. Leeson. She died at Lutterworth in March 1978 aged eighty-one.

A tram decorated for victory at the end of the First World War.

Conductresses among the staff of the Leicester Tram Company. The second on the right in the back row is Mrs A. Leeson.

Laying the tram lines at the clock tower, *c.* 1904. The tram company had about 50 trams and 230 horses when it first started. The central headquarters occupied nearly an acre of ground between Humberstone Gate and Belgrave Gate. The electric tram service started on 18 May 1904 and finished on 9 November 1949.

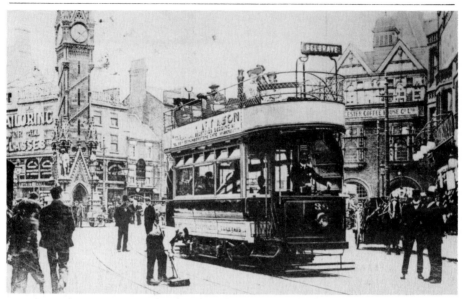
Open-topped tram No. 30 at the clock tower, ready for Belgrave, *c.* 1930.

Laying the tram lines at the clock tower. The city obviously came to a standstill.

Great Central station, *c.* 1925. A very busy 5 p.m. according to the clock tower. In 1916 the station master was John Richard Tebb. Dean & Dawson Ltd of 1 Gallowtree Gate were the booking agents as well as the station office.

109 Central Station, Leicester

Great Central station, *c.* 1910. This shows the Parcels Office entrance. The passenger
entrance is further down on the left.

The GNR Open Day at Belgrave Road station, May 1882. In 1916 the station master
here was Stephen Bee and passengers booked at 35 Gallowtree Gate as well as the station.

The Midland station, London Road, seen here *c.* 1920, was built in 1892 by C. Trubshaw. In 1916 Richard W. Mapp was the station master and bookings were made at Cook & Sons office in Gallowtree Gate as well as at the station.

Midland Railway station, London Road, *c.* 1903.

Horsefair Street, *c.* 1940. The Town Hall is on the left, the Royal Hotel on the right and beyond is the Theatre Royal. The theatre was built in 1836 by W. Parsons. Mr Thomas Moxon of High Street was instrumental in saving it for the people of Leicester when it was the only theatre for drama. He was presented with a silver tankard on 15 February 1848. Famous names like Ray Mort and Billie Whitelaw played here.

SECTION SIX

Churches

St Mary's, seen here from West Bridge, stands on a hill beside the Grand Union Canal where many industrial buildings were sited, *c.* 1930. Donisthorpe & Co. were founded here in 1739. The river and canal provided both power and transport.

St Mary's church and the Castle Gateway, *c.* 1918, an oasis of peace and quiet in the centre of Leicester.

St. Mary's Church and Castle, Leicester.

St Mary's church and the Castle seen from the river, *c.* 1920. The supposed date of the church is 1107.

St Margaret's church, *c.* 1910. Some parts of this building date back to the thirteenth century, but it was altered, improved and renovated by Scott and Street in 1860 and 1880. It has one of the grandest Perpendicular towers in Leicestershire.

St Mary's church, *c.* 1910. The picture shows Prince Rupert's Archway. The sign on the left is for Shipley Stonemasons.

St James' church seen from Victoria Park, *c.* 1905. St James the Greater church was built in 1899–1901 by H.L. Goddard, but only finally completed in 1914.

St Denys' church, Evington, *c.* 1900. This was mostly built in the late thirteenth century. To the west of the church are earthwork remains of the memorial complex known as Piggy's Hollow.

St Paul's church, at the junction of Glenfield Road and Kirby Road (*c.* 1910), was built by Ordish and Traylen in 1870 from Mountsorrell granite. A spire was proposed but never added.

Melbourne Hall, *c.* 1900, and Revd B.J. Gibbon. This Evangelical Free church was built in 1880–1 by Goddard & Paget in a simple Gothic style using red brick.

St Mark's church, *c.* 1905, and Revd F.L. Donaldson. The church was built in 1870–2 by Ewan Christian and the west end added by E.C. Shearman in 1903. It was a gift from W. Perry Herrick of Beaumanor Park.

St George's church at the height of the fire in October 1911 which almost completely destroyed it. It is not known if the new church is a good copy of the original which was built in 1827.

St Nicholas' church, *c.* 1910, and Revd E. Atkins. This was originally in Sycamore Lane, which ran from Blue Boar Lane to Friars Causeway. The lane disappeared when the Great Central station was built.

St Mary's church, *c.* 1910. This has been rebuilt so many times it is difficult to put a real date on it, but there was a chapel on the site in 1107. The founder was Robert de Beaumont, first Earl of Leicester. The spire was rebuilt in 1785.

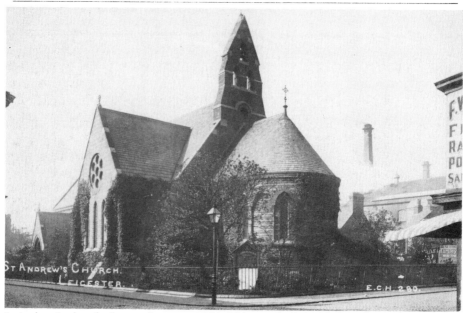

St Andrew's church, Jarrom Street, *c.* 1911. This was built in 1862 in the Gothic style by G.G. Scott who also built the vicarage.

Westcotes Drive pictured from Narborough Road, *c.* 1920, and showing the tower of the Church of the Martyrs built in 1889.

St Mary's church, Humberstone, *c.* 1940. It was rebuilt in 1857 by Raphael Brandon, although some of the church may be post-medieval. Some find the very unusual spire ugly.

Inside the church (*c.* 1940) there is much to interest the visitor: pretty terracotta flowers, richly decorated font and the stained-glass windows by Hardman.

Holy Trinity Church, Leicester

Holy Trinity church in Regent Road, built originally in 1838 by S. Smirke, remodelled in 1871 by S.S. Teulon, and seen here *c.* 1910. A very unusual looking church for its time.

De Montford Street, Leicester

A sunlit De Montfort Street and the spire of St Stephen's church, *c.* 1920.

Parks

Victoria Park, *c.* 1910. The Pavilion was destroyed by a land mine on 20 November 1940.

Another view of Victoria Park, the avenue of trees and the wrought iron arbour, *c.* 1900.

The tennis courts and war memorial, *c.* 1927. This postcard was sent on 11 October 1927 from 66 Barclay Street, the home of Mr Joseph Knight, a police constable.

Part of the crowd of onlookers at the pageant in Victoria Park on Coronation Day, 22 June 1911.

The Victoria Park Gates and Lodges, as well as the war memorial, were given to the city by Sir Jonathan North and designed by Lutyens.

The bandstand behind the ill-fated Pavilion, *c.* 1910.

Victoria Park was laid out in 1883 on what had been the old racecourse.

Abbey Park on a tranquil Sunday afternoon, *c.* 1925. The café is in the background. 'Tudorbethan' lodges were built in 1881 by Tait.

Abbey Park Ruins, *c.* 1920. The Abbey of St Mary of the Meadows lay to the north of St Margaret's. It was founded in 1143 by Robert Le Bossu for canons of the order of St Augustine. Some twenty to thirty canons lived here.

THE LAKE, ABBEY PARK, LEICESTER.

02177

Abbey Park Lake, with its swans and ducks, provides a quiet walk in the peace of the abbey but with one of the hosiery industry's chimneys in the background, *c.* 1917.

Abbey Park contains some sixty acres of land laid out in 1882 and opened by the Prince and Princess of Wales.

Abbey Bridge, Abbey Park, *c.* 1935. When the park was laid out by Barron & Son in 1878–82, as part of the municipal flood works, the River Soar was lowered and widened to form a lake.

The Pavilion in Abbey Park was a fine looking building, with beautiful flower and rose gardens on the approach, *c.* 1925.

The Sunday afternoon fashion show at the Western Park Gates, *c.* 1900. These gates must have been the first. All I can remember are the very tall wrought iron gates. There was an army depot just inside on the left which became King Richard III School for Boys after the Second World War. Mr Shalifour was headmaster and members of staff included Mr W. Culsey, Mr Johnson, Mr Oldham and Mr Starmer. With Malcolm and Barry Richards of Winchester Avenue and others, I played the violin as part of 'The Ricardians' band.

The Headley tea room, Western Park, 1905.

The main driveway through Western Park, c. 1906, before the bowling greens and the cpen-air school where one Miss Kitty Stead taught.

Part of the crowd celebrating the 1911 coronation in Western Park. The hat manufacturers must have had a field day. It is rare to see such a crowd assembled today for peaceful purposes.

Western Park, *c.* 1900. The Park Farm buildings are on the left, on the right is the main house which was to become Headleys Café.

Western Park, *c.* 1930. The bandstand is on the hill. My memories are of sledging down over the bridge and across the road. Sometimes we jumped the stream (which has now been filled in).

A view looking down on the new bowling greens and across to the tea rooms in Western Park, *c.* 1909.

Tennis courts and bowling greens in Western Park, *c.* 1930. The children's slide and roundabout are in the background.

Humberstone Park boating lake, *c.* 1940.

J.H. Headley, Caterer, Teas and Refreshments, Western Park Tea Rooms. The pace of life was slower in 1920, gentlefolk took afternoon tea and time stood still. Mrs Polly Headley was the baker.

Spinney Hill Park cricket match, *c.* 1920. It would be interesting to know the teams and the score.

Spinney Hill Park Pavilion, *c.* 1916. An oasis of calm in a busy city.

The new pavilion at Spinney Hill Park, *c.* 1930. A lovely old perambulator of the time may be seen. I seem to remember we had one like it.

Castle Gardens, *c.* 1940, was a place in which to reflect on business in the heart of a bustling city and beside the River Soar.

Westcotes Gardens, *c.* 1920. Country mansions like Westcotes Hall were destroyed as the new Leicester was created.

Westcotes Gardens, *c.* 1910. Laid out between Upperton Road and Ashleigh Road, this was at one time part of the Westcotes Estate.

SECTION EIGHT
Around and About

High Cross Street, *c.* 1830. Two new gaols were built in High Cross Street in 1792, the Welford Road gaol in 1828. A market was held at the Cross on Wednesdays. Public announcements were made and executions took place here.

Map of Leicester in 1928 before the first industrial expansion. Abbey Meadows is at the top; St Margarets Fields at bottom right; the clock tower is in the centre.

The Clock Tower, *c.* 1920, looking towards Eastgates and the junction of Cheapside.

The Clock Tower, *c.* 1907, showing an open-top tram, John Burton & Sons, and Dean & Dawson Tours and Booking Agents.

Eastgate, *c.* 1925. This picture is taken from the bottom of High Street/Silver Street. Tram and bus passengers stood at this spot to await the Hinckley Road and Narborough Road transport.

Gallowtree Gate, *c.* 1920. On the left is the Maypole Dairy. The tram is destined for the Midland station. Gallowtree Gate was where executions took place.

High Street, *c.* 1900, with Lloyds Bank on the right. In 1916 Edward L. Mylius was the manager.

Highfield Street, *c.* 1910, with one set of tram lines. The girls are on their way to school, or to one of the many piano teachers, deportment classes or elocutionists.

High Street, looking down towards the clock tower, *c.* 1890. The tower on the left was Huntingdon Tower Buildings, a swine market until 1902. Most of the shops in this area, as well as the tower, were pulled down for road widening.

High Street, *c.* 1922. On the right are the Singer Sewing Machine Company, Arthur Lowe, fruiterer, John Adams, ironmonger, William Henry Nott, tailor, and Butler's chemists.

High Street, *c.* 1930. The queue of trams waiting to go round the clock tower was a regular sight. Lloyds Bank is in the background.

Huntingdon Tower, near the corner of Union Street, *c.* 1890.

High Street, *c.* 1930, showing the Hare and Pheasant public house, Smith's clothing store and Roberts & Roberts' grocers.

Huntingdon Tower, *c.* 1890. Lords Place is the relic of an Elizabethan town house of the Earl of Huntingdon. It was last used by Mr George Richardson, a bootmaker, but was pulled down when High Street was widened, *c.* 1900.

High Street, looking towards the clock tower, *c.* 1930. The Co-Operative store is on the left. A. Whitcher & Co. Limited's 'The Magnet' is further down and the Cameo News Theatre, known then as the Imperial Playhouse, is on the right.

Eastgate, looking up High Street and Silver Street, *c.* 1930. Crowes Ltd were drapers, milliners and furnishers.

Belgrave Gate, *c.* 1903, from a postcard sent to Holland on 29 December 1903 by a visitor to the Grand Hotel.

Belgrave Road, *c.* 1910. The confectionery and hardware shop at No. 168 on the left was owned by Mrs Annie Louisa Jones.

Humberstone Gate, *c.* 1900. A motor car gets in the way of a tram. The general opinion at the time was that the reverse was more likely to occur.

Humberstone Gate on a very busy day in the centre of Leicester, *c.* 1910. The building on the right contained The Fox Hotel, Gollands Confectioners, G. Bonser, hairdresser, dress shops, and a saddlers. All were pulled down to make way for the Lewis building.

Humberstone Gate, at a point lower down than in the previous picture, *c.* 1910. The Wyggeston Grammar School for Girls is on the left. Behind the trees is Challis & Allen, wine and spirit merchants.

Humberstone Gate, *c.* 1900, showing the Craven Arms Hotel with various horse-drawn vehicles outside. The publican was Frederick Charles Woodbridge. Next door was the Leicester Corporation Tramways Depot with manager A.F. Lucas.

Humberstone Gate, *c.* 1940. The last street fair in Humberstone Gate was held in 1904. The Stag and Pheasant Inn was on the left.

Gallowtree Gate, *c.* 1920. On the left are Horniman's Pipes, advertised on the sun blind of Newmans the tobacconists, the Pelican (Walter Spriggs the landlord) and Gee-Nephew & Co. Ltd. On the right are the Black Boy Chocolates shop, Richard Jones, outfitter (before they moved), and artificial teeth manufacturer Lloyd Bros, owned by Mr N. Simmons.

Gallowtree Gate, *c.* 1930. The policeman is on point duty on his box. F.W. Woolworth's proudly advertises 'nothing over sixpence': those were the days!

Granby Street, *c.* 1903. A busy day, but not a car in sight – just people, carts, horses, cycles and a boy with a home-made truck.

Granby Street (*c.* 1903), the heart of commerce. The post office, the National Provincial Bank of England, the library, architects, solicitors and the Groby Granite Co. registered office were all here.

Granby Street, *c.* 1940 – how different from today. The policeman on duty, the Roneo shop – what a skyline!

Another lovely picture of the middle section of Granby Street, *c.* 1924. No. 16 on the left was Fred Rainey Godrich's tobacconists. Also shown is Kendall & Sons, umbrella makers. (I remember Mr C. Mayes who worked in the factory.)

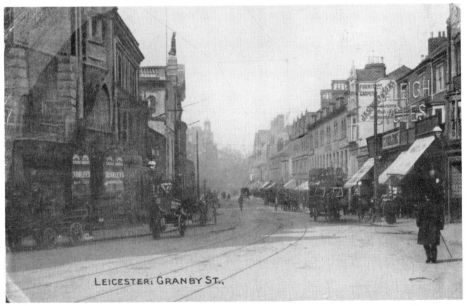

The top end of Granby Street, *c.* 1908. On the right was H.H. Burton, the jewellers. It is interesting to note that a company called F. Dolton & Sons had their talking machine depot at No. 76!

Granby Street, looking in the opposite direction from the previous picture, *c.* 1912. On the right was the Wellington Hotel, on the left the King's Restaurant, started in 1898. Further down was the post office.

A good view of the corner and tower of The Grand Hotel, Granby Street, *c.* 1900. On the top floor on the left is the Spirella Corsetier Madame Waterman, and on the floor below John H. Rickert, dentist. On the ground floor is Geo. A. Draycott, fruiterer.

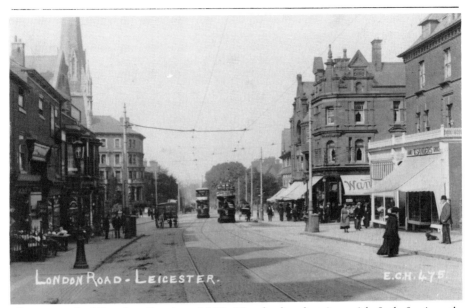

The top end of London Road, *c.* 1910. Wands the chemist, with Seth Squires the manager, is on the corner of Highfield Street. On the other corner is the milliners C.E. & M.E. Hulme. Next is William Sanders, the grocers.

Another fine view of the top of London Road, *c.* 1910, with an advertisement for the Palace Theatre and the Victoria Baptist church.

Hilltop, London Road, outside the Victoria Park, showing Mill Hill Lane and Mill Hill School, *c.* 1904. The children are waiting for the tram.

Market Place, *c.* 1918, from the top of Halford Street. The Corn Exchange in the market place is clearly seen.

PLACE, LEICESTER

Market Place, *c.* 1920. This card was sent to Sgt G. Smith (1016), 1/5 Yorks & Lancs Regiment, Clipstone Camp, Nottingham, from Jim, K2 Ward, 5 Northern General Base Hospital, Leics, and was one of many sent by wounded soldiers asking for a visit. A very important improvement took place in 1876 with the opening of a new entrance to the Market Place from Granby Street. This was needed because of the large number of people attending the cheese and wool markets.

Market Place, *c.* 1905. This view looks towards the rear of premises occupied at one time by Simpkin & James, one of the better grocers.

The Corn Exchange, c. 1896. The ground floor was built by William Flint in 1850 as the Exchange. The upper floor was added as temporary housing for the magistracy. In the centre of the picture is the statue of the Duke of Rutland by Edward Davis. The bridge in front of the Corn Exchange, designed by Mr Ord, has been described on numerous occasions as 'The Rialto'.

The Leicester Unemployment March from the Market Place in front of the Corn Exchange to London on 4 June 1905. In the background is the sixpence-halfpenny bazaar in the Silver Arcade.

Market Place, *c.* 1908, showing Adderley & Co., Gee-Nephew Co. Ltd, etc. Some of the buildings in the Market Place are seventeenth century. The cast iron fish market is Victorian (1881).

Market Place, *c.* 1920. This card was sent to an address in Shrewsbury by Annie and Harrold of 67 Sylvan Street, Leicester. The market stalls all had canvas tops.

Horsefair Street, looking up towards the town hall, *c.* 1907. On the left is the National Provincial Bank. The Three Crowns public house used to be here but was demolished in 1870. The last stagecoach left here in 1866.

A memorial procession for the late King Edward VII, 20 May 1910, in Greyfriars.

Market Street, *c.* 1940. A few names I remember from days past include Joseph Johnson (where I once worked), William Oliver, the Midland Educational Co., Kunzle the confectioner and Herringtons, the ladies' shop.

Belvoir Street, *c.* 1900. The first building on the right is the city lending library, built in 1831 by William Flint as a meeting hall for Liberals. The next building is the Belvoir Street Baptist chapel, built in 1845 and better known as the 'Pork Pie' chapel.

Municipal Buildings, *c.* 1916. The town hall was built in 1874–6 by F.J. Hames, one of the first Queen Anne-style municipal buildings. It cost £53,000 to build and took two years. The foundation stone was laid on August Bank Holiday 1874.

The bronze fountain with four winged lions in Town Hall Square, *c.* 1910. Designed by F.J. Hames, constructed in 1879 and presented to the town by Councellor Israel Hart, it cost £1,200.

The Temperance Hall, *c.* 1920.

Horsefair Street, *c.* 1900. The Theatre Royal, built in 1836, is on the left. It was demolished in 1956. The clock tower is part of the town hall.

The Grand Hotel, *c.* 1916, showing the optologists, Charnley & Sons, at No. 39 and the hairdresser, William Preston, at No. 43. Readers may remember the three shops of Knight's, the outfitters. I had the privilege of working for Mr K.K. Knight, along with Mr George Moore, Mr O. Gibson, Mr Peter Bull, Mr B. Warner, Mr P. Knott, Mr Roy Finn and Mr R. Lait, in 1952

Municipal Library, *c.* 1907.

The statue of John Biggs outside the Leicestershire Club, Welford Place, *c.* 1900.

A memorial service for Edward VII in the Market Place, 20 May 1910.

March to London against food shortage and unemployment, 1908.

Leicester Royal Infirmary, c. 1911, on a postcard sent to Miss Skerritt at Saxby by Ada of Leicester. On 7 October 1767 subscribers accepted Richard Walker's (of Little Stretton) offer of Chaple Close (Southgate Street). The deed of sale is dated 24 September 1768, and the price was £525 for about five acres. At one time the nurses had part of a house in Aylestone Road, but in 1887 the nurses' home was completed as an extension of Apreece wing.

The photo is by William Pell of Bosworth Street, Leicester. After fifteen years of deliberation the local board of health finally built the Isolation Hospital in 1870. There were several arguments about who should look after fracture cases if they had fevers as well, but in 1882, following a typhoid outbreak among the nurses, all was resolved. The new Isolation Hospital in Groby Road opened in 1900. The card was posted on 3 January 1907.

No. 24 High Cross Street, on the corner of Thornton Lane. This was the tobacconists and newsagents run by Mr Edgar Woods. He lived on the premises with his wife and three daughters, known by some as the 'splinters'. He died in 1990 aged ninety-four, having spent his retirement in Syston. Prior to running the High Cross Street business he was manager of the Home & Colonial in St Nicholas Street.

High Cross Street, when No. 24 was a hosiers. The building on the right, the Golden Lion public house, was demolished in 1869 for the new Everards estate.

The open-top tram to Victoria Park, at the junction of Knighton Park Road with Victoria Park Road East, *c*. 1906.

The Castle, seen from the Newarke Bridge, *c*. 1930. It was begun in around 1100 by Hugh de Grentmesnil. Early in the thirteenth century it was owned by Simon de Montfort. It has been altered and rebuilt so many times that it is difficult to know what it looked like originally.

The Museum, *c.* 1920. This postcard was sent from 19 West Street, Leicester, 'with love from Gracie', to Burnham-on-Sea. The Museum was converted from a preparatory school in 1849.

New Walk, *c.* 1917. A fine view of this popular walk, with pedestrians quite unaware of the camera.

A tree-lined New Walk on a dark December morning.

Leicester Museum, c. 1920, showing New Walk on a quiet day. The Leicester coat of arms has been superimposed on this fine postcard.

HM Prison, Welford Road, *c.* 1916. The governor at this time was John Thomas Noon, Richard Adolphus Gibbs was steward and the matron was Miss Mary Emma Hulse. Thomas Brown was chief warder. It was built in 1825–8 by W. Parsons, the county surveyor. The governor's house was built in 1844–6.

Newarke Gateway, *c.* 1925. Built in 1410, it was left stranded in the middle of the road in the early 1900s. It was used as a military magazine during the Civil War and as a corner of the drill square in 1894.

'The Magazine', *c.* 1925.

Another view of the Newarke Gateway, *c.* 1910, one of the many military buildings in Leicester.

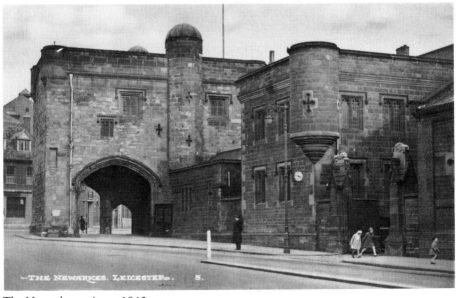

The Newarke again, *c.* 1943.

Prince Rupert's Gateway, *c.* 1910, named after Prince Rupert, who pounded the Newarke walls for two days in 1645 and sent in his troops once they were breached.

The Jewry Wall, *c.* 1910, a part of one wall of the Basilica, which was in turn part of the complex of public Roman buildings comprising the Basilica, the Baths and the Forum. Its close proximity to St Nicholas' church has helped to preserve it.

Castle Gateway, *c.* 1904. The Castle was begun in around 1100 by Hugh de Grentmesnil and rebuilt by Robert de Beaumont. It stands in a prominent position above the River Soar.

The house in St Nicholas Street (*c.* 1904) where Bunyan and Wesley took lodgings.

Braunstone Gate, *c.* 1909. The shop on the left is that of James Edward Jordan, a secondhand bookseller. The shop on the right belonged to Mrs Emily Hurlbut, an umbrella maker.

Hinckley Road, *c.* 1908. The public house on the right is the Hinckley Road Brewery. The manager was Mr Carter Crossland.

The junction of Narborough Road and Upperton Road, *c.* 1904. The Narborough Road school, Westcotes, is on the corner. The advertisement on the tram is for 'Gallard Corsets'.

Narborough Road. Leicester,

Narborough Road, *c.* 1910. The picture is taken from the junction with Hinckley Road. The building on the left is the Westcotes Mission Room.

Hinckley Road looking from the Josse. Leicester.

Hinckley Road, *c.* 1904. The Methodist church stands on the corner. A misprint reads 'the Josse'. This, of course, is the Fosse Way.

Hinckley Road, Leicester.

Hinckley Road, *c.* 1910. A tram approaches the Fosse Road crossroads. The Methodist chapel is just visible on the right.

The Queen Street fire of 5 October 1911. St George's church was also burnt down.

A First World War margarine queue outside the Home & Colonial in the Market Place.

A well-known spot in old Leicester, the railway crossing above the canal on Western Boulevard. The Kirby & West Dairy is in the background on the right. This area was known by tram passengers as the 'five lights' because of the lamp standard on the central island.

Castle Street, off Southgate Street, at West Bridge, *c.* 1895. The postcard shows the old bakehouse run by Miss Perkins which was pulled down in 1910.

Clarendon Park, *c.* 1910. William T. Hind of 78 Queens Road is on the right-hand corner.

Near the boathouse at Aylestone Bridge, *c.* 1920. Rowing was a popular Sunday afternoon pastime. We used to swim there in the summer.

Aylestone Road Floods, December 1910. The Leicester Gas Company purchased thirty-four acres of land in 1877 and built the gasworks. This was largely the work of three men, Aldermen Grimsley, Stafford and Winterton (the then mayor). In 1829 gas cost 12s. per 1,000 sq. ft, but in 1877 it cost 2s. 10d.

Aylestone Gas Works, *c.* 1905, now the Emgas service centre. The row of three-storey cottages was built for the gas workers in 1879. The manager's house is next to the clock tower. The works superintendent in 1916 was Mr E. Frost.

Aylestone Road, looking back towards the city from near the cattle market, *c.* 1920.

Tram No. 48 at the terminus at Aylestone, *c.* 1905. The conductor is seen reversing the pickup pole.

Belgrave, described here as the New Bridge, *c.* 1910.

Belgrave village from Stocking Farm, *c.* 1900.

The tram terminus at Loughborough Road, *c.* 1915.

The Old Bridge, Belgrave. This bridge spanned the River Soar on the Thurcaston Road in Roman times.

Tramcar turnings – what memories! The pole on the roof of the tramcar clipped onto the overhead wires. There was a long bamboo pole stored at each terminus on a lamp post and this was used by the conductor to reverse the direction of the tramcar. The conductor would then push the back of one of the seats and they would all end up facing the other way. The postcard shows Uppingham Road.

The New Tollgate, Loughborough Road, which was situated at the tram terminus. The tolls were abolished in 1878.

Mowmacre Hill, Belgrave, *c.* 1900. In 1842 a great assembly of framework knitters in Leicester Market Place occurred. Chartists numbering 1,500 met at Humberstone Gate and marched to Belgrave. The police were called and a fracas ensued. This later became known as the battle of Mowmacre Hill.

Thurcaston Road, Belgrave, *c.* 1920.

Checketts Road, *c.*1900, was a very busy road. The Corn, Hay and Straw Merchants shows how near to the countryside this once was.

The corner of Checketts Road and Loughborough Road, *c.* 1910. On the right is the Champion Hotel (Alfred Ford was the owner). On the far corner is the tobacconists owned by Mr Geo. Bennett which doubled as the Midland Railway parcels office.

Old Humberstone Village, *c.* 1907, described in 1916 as a parish and pleasant village about half a mile from Humberstone station.

Humberstone Hall, *c*. 1904. Formerly known as the Manor House, in 1916 this was the home of Sir Maurice Levy Bt, Member of Parliament and a Justice of the Peace. The hall had been enlarged in 1789.

The Humber Stone was in a field on the right-hand side of Thurcaston Lane, now part of the Hamilton estate. At one time it stood five feet tall but a farmer knocked it down because of the nuisance to his tractors. He was ruined. It is said to bring bad luck to anyone who touches it.

This thatched cottage was the home of the groom at Humberstone Hall. It stands at the corner of Main Street and Tennis Court Drive. It has what are known as 'poachin' chimneys.

Two trams in Fosse Road North, *c.* 1920. The second tram advertises S.T. Grant and Son, furnishers in the Haymarket.

Tram No. 6 passing under the railway bridge on Fosse Road North, *c.* 1930. The bridge is no longer there.

St Andrew's church in Jarrom Street, built in 1860 by G.G. Scott and seen here in around 1907.

Bolton Road, *c.* 1910. One of the seven shops in Bolton Road which belonged to Percy W. Bambury.

Minehead Street, *c.* 1920, like Dunster Street, Taunton Avenue and Dulverton Road, is named after a Somerset town.

Kirby Road, looking down towards St Paul's church, *c.* 1904.

Gimson Road, *c.* 1921. John Hudson, the market gardener, lived here, and the new Co-Operative Dairy was built at the top on the right.

Dulverton Road, *c.* 1920. Mr Fredk W. Pallet of Pallett Bros, the paper bag manufacturers, lived at No. 59. They moved to Wyngate Drive in the 1930s.

Muriel Road, *c.* 1907. Muriel Road connects Glenfield Road to Kirby Road. The group of people is believed to be outside No. 38. On the right hand side are Kirby and West Dairymen.

Wartime

A Dover Street fire started by incendiary bombs, *c.* 1940, spread to the Arthur Kemp Ltd factory with disastrous results.

A German map of Leicester used during the Second World War and showing possible targets. It was captured on a German airfield in Belgium in 1945 by Bernard Fawkes of Wymondham and presented to Trevor Hickman by Mrs Fawkes in 1987.

Bomb damage and a gas main fire in Cavendish Road, 21 August 1940.

Bomb damage in Frank Street, 19 November 1940.

Cavendish Road, August 1940, the first blow on Leicester. Twenty-four people were injured and six killed.

Essex Road, just off Gipsy Lane, 14 September 1940. Four people were killed by one bomb.

Squires in Narborough Road, 14 November 1940. The well-known bakers was extensively damaged by a string of bombs dropped from Aylestone Road to King Richard's Road.

Several houses were demolished in the Humberstone Road/Frank Street area. Many lives were lost.

Forty-one people lost their lives when a bomb fell on the junction of Tichborne Street and Highfield Street.

Ten lives were lost and many were injured in Grove Road, *c.* 1940. The St Saviours Road area was the scene of much suffering.

Men of the 14th Battalion, Leicestershire Regiment, formed in 1918. This photograph was taken at Tantignies in November 1918. Among the men are E.H. Butler, G.A. Bliss, E.R. Angrave, P.W. Walder and C.H. Elson.

Warrant officer and NCOs of the 10th Leicester Regiment, *c.* 1920.

The Pavilion in Victoria Park, demolished by a land mine on 20 November 1940. Although known to all sportsmen, the building was not greatly missed by many.

Freeman, Hardy & Willis after the fire in 1940. During the bombing many people were killed and properties ruined. The picture was taken from Humberstone Road.

Damage caused by the raid on Cavendish Road on 21 August 1940. It was possibly aimed at the gasworks.

Acknowledgements

Many people have helped with pictures and text, and I thank them for this, but special thanks must go to Annie and Stuart Burton for deciphering and typing my scribble. Thanks also to Trevor Hickman for his knowledge of publishing, and to Nicholas Corah, June Harris, Kitty Head, Brian Chawner, Ann and Michael Potter, Les Hart, Andrew Charles, Eddie Cuss, Mike Kellett of K & S Commerial Photos Limited, the *Leicester Mercury* and Robin Jenkins and staff of the Archives Department at the Leicester Museum for photographs, postcards and advice. And, last but not least, to Beryl my wife, who put up with my moods and late nights while I endeavoured to complete this book. To all I say thank you.

David R. Burton